GUINEA PIGS

Sandie Lee Books

Guinea Pigs

The first guinea pigs were domesticated (tamed) around 5,000 BC. They were bred for the purpose of food. Today, there are many breeds of this animal. They are kept as pets and used in laboratories for medical research. Despite its name, these animals are not related to the pig. They are considered a rodent and are in the family of the, Caviidae. Let's take a journey through the world of guinea pigs to discover more cool and fascinating facts.

Where in the World?

Did you know the guinea pig originated in the Andes in South America? This animal was introduced as a pet in the 16th century. European traders brought this animal back with them and began breeding the guinea pig. Now this animal is a common pet found in homes all over the world.

Guinea Pigs in the Wild

Did you know there are still guinea pigs living in the wild? These wild cavies can be found on grassy plains. These animals are very social and live in small groups. This group can have several females, 1 male and their young. Some of the wild guinea pigs are thought to have been once domesticated, but were returned to the wild.

The Body of a Guinea Pig

Did you know this animal does not have a tail? Guinea pigs can measure up to 9.8 inches long and weigh around 2.6 pounds. Their bodies are more stocky than they are long. These animals also have 2 black beady eyes, long front teeth and somewhat large, round ears.

What the Guinea Pig Eats

Did you know this animal likes to eat all the time? A guinea pig in the wild will eat grass, stems, shoots and seeds. If you keep a guinea pig as a pet, you can buy pre-packaged seeds and pellets for it. The guinea pig also enjoys eating hay. This can be used as bedding, too!

The Guinea Pig's Special

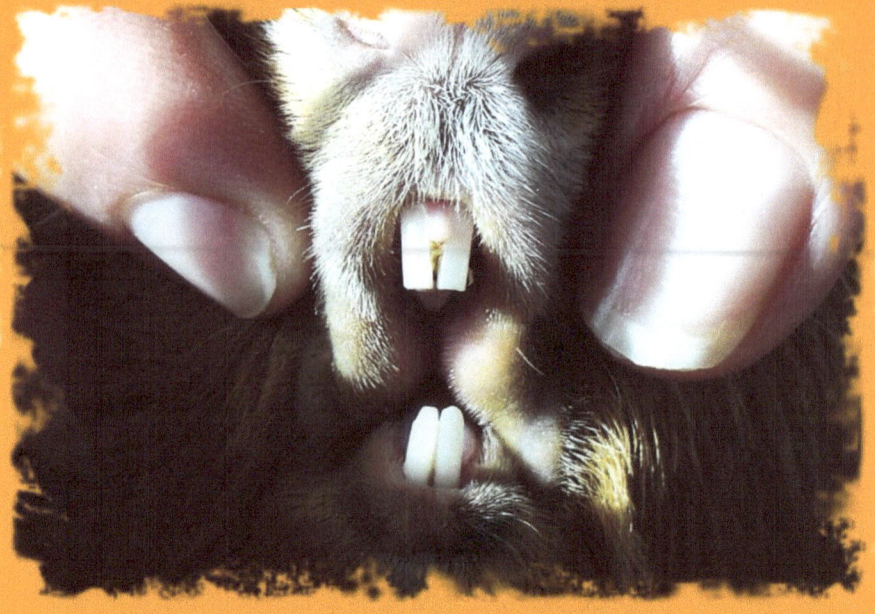

Did you know this animal's teeth never stop growing? This is called being open rooted. If you were to look inside this animal's mouth, you would see two sets of teeth. A pair of long chompers on top and another pair on the bottom. The guinea pig has to chew on tough things to keep its teeth from overgrowing.

The Guinea Pig as Prey

Did you know in the wild, guinea pigs have natural predators? Since this rodent is so small, it is only logical that it would be hunted. Land predators such as snakes, wild cats and wolves hunt this animal. Large predatory birds like eagles and hawks will also catch and dine on the guinea pig.

The Guinea Pig as a Pet

Did you know the guinea pig makes a great pet? This animal is a very popular pet. It is friendly and easy to handle. To keep a guinea pig as a pet, you will need a large cage, a water bottle, food and food dish and bedding for the bottom of its cage.

Guinea Pig Talk

Did you know this animal makes a lot of different sounds? Wheeking is a long sound. This is done when your guinea pig is excited. A purring guinea pig is content. Teeth chatter and growling means this animal is upset. A shrieking sound means the guinea pig is scared or in pain.

Mom Guinea Pig

Did you know the female guinea pig is called, a sow? Mom guinea pig can have up to 5 litters each year. She will carry her young for around 72 days. The litter size can be from 1 to 6 babies. When pregnant, the female gets very big and fat - like an eggplant!

Baby Guinea Pigs

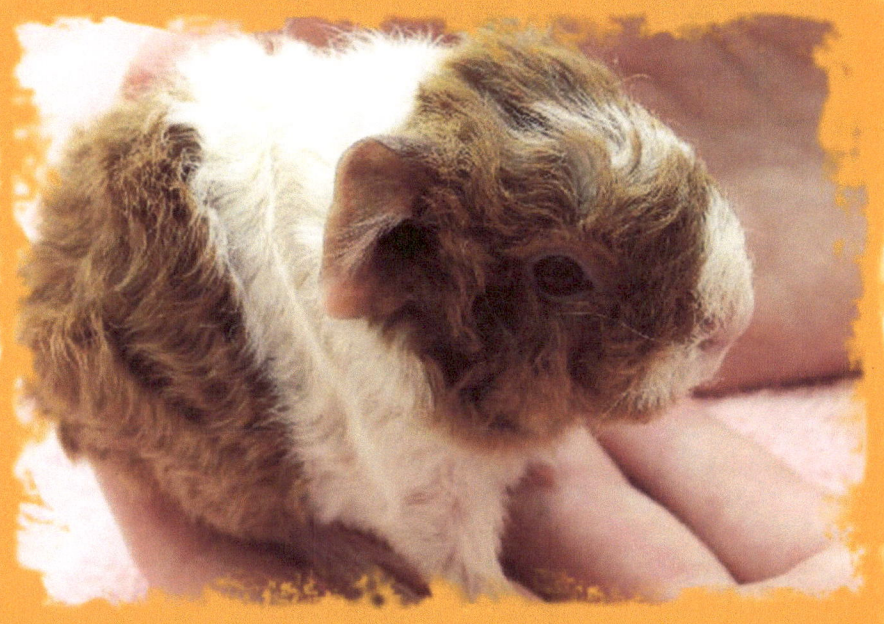

Did you know baby guinea pigs are called, pups? Unlike other animals, the pup is born with hair, teeth, claws and can even see a little bit. The baby guinea pig can walk around shortly after birth. Even though the pup suckles milk from mom, it is able to eat solid food, as well.

Life of a Guinea Pig

Did you know the guinea pig is crepuscular? This means it is active during the early dawn and at dusk. The wild guinea pig spends its time moving with its group. It will continuously eat and will seek shelter in crevices or tunnels. As a pet, you can expect your guinea pig to live from 4 to 5 years of age.

Long Coated Guinea Pigs

As the name suggests, this type of guinea pig has a very long smooth coat It can get so long, that it will be difficult for this animal to walk around. This guinea pig is usually kept as a show pet. This means the guinea pig will be judged by the length and quality of its coat.

Rough Coated Guinea Pigs

This type of guinea pig has short hair with rosettes. The hair will stick out with a definite center spot where you can see its skin. The rosettes will be all over its body; 1 on each shoulder, 4 across its back, 1 on each hip and 2 on its rump.

Hairless Guinea Pigs

This breed of the guinea pig is virtually bald. This guinea pig needs to be kept very warm and dry. It will also need an energy-rich food to keep it in top condition. The Baldwin breed of the hairless guinea pig is born with a full coat. But it later falls out as this animal ages.

Quiz

Question 1: When was the first guinea pig domesticated?

Answer 1: Around 5,000 BC

Question 2: What doesn't the guinea pig have?

Answer 2: A tail

Question 3: What body part never stops growing on the guinea pig?

Answer 3: Its teeth

Question 4: What is wheeking?

Answer 4: A long sound the guinea
pig makes

Question 5: The guinea pig is *crepuscular*. What does this mean?

Answer 5: It is most active in the early morning and at dusk

Thank you for checking out another addition from Sandie Lee Books! Make sure to check out Amazon.com for many other great titles.